General Instruction

Plastic Canvas

The sample projects shown were stitched on Darice plastic canvas.

For stability and durability, the fronts and backs are stitched on stiff plastic canvas; the sides, bases and smaller pieces are stitched on regular clear 7-count plastic canvas. Some designs use pieces cut from plastic canvas shapes, like circles, hearts and stars.

Fibers

The sample projects shown were stitched using Uniek Needloft plastic canvas yarn. Some designs also feature Madeira GlissenGloss metallic braid ribbon and/or DMC 6-strand cotton embroidery floss.

When stitching with metallic braid ribbon, feed it between your thumb and finger so that it lies flat.

When adding details using embroidery floss, use all 6 strands of floss unless instructed otherwise. For even coverage, separate the strands from a length of floss, then recombine the correct number without twisting before threading them onto the needle.

A #16 tapestry needle is recommended for stitching with plastic canvas yarn. A #18 tapestry needle is recommended for stitching with the metallic braid ribbon. Smaller needles—#20, #22, #24—are recommended for adding details with embroidery floss. Feel free to use the size needle that works best for you.

Optional Reinforced Handles

If you are tucking something weighty into your finished gift tote, consider reinforcing the tote handles with a second layer of plastic canvas. Especially on the Kitty Cat, Santa and Winter Snowman designs, where the handles are cut as part of the tote front and back, too much stress could cause the handles to tear at the point where they meet the tote front and back.

Use the graph as a pattern to cut a reinforcing piece for each handle from stiff plastic canvas. The reinforcement should include the entire handle and an inch or so of the design across the top edge of the tote front and back.

Hold the reinforcement against the wrong side of the plastic canvas and work through both layers as you stitch. Or, Whipstitch it to the tote when you Whipstitch and Overcast the edges and assemble the tote.

Bunny in the Garden

Size: 7½ inches W x 9¾ inches H x 3¼ inches D (19cm x 24.8cm x 8.2cm) excluding handles
Skill Level: Beginner

Materials

- ❑ 7-count plastic canvas from Darice:
  - 1 sheet clear regular
  - 2 artist-size sheets (12-inch x 18-inch/ 30.5cm x 45.7cm) stiff
- ❑ Uniek Needloft plastic canvas yarn as listed in color key
- ❑ DMC 6-strand embroidery floss as listed in color key
- ❑ Tapestry needles: #16, #18
- ❑ Hot-glue gun

Stitching Step by Step

1 *Cut plastic canvas according to graphs:* Cut two sides and handles from regular, and two head front/back pieces and two body front/back pieces from stiff.

2 From regular plastic canvas, also cut one piece 49 holes x 20 holes for tote bottom; tote bottom will remain unstitched.

3 Stitch body front and back according to graph, leaving unstitched areas as noted, and referring to stitch diagrams to work Turkey Loop Stitches where indicated for bunny tails.

4 Stitch head front/back and sides according to graphs, filling in uncoded areas with white Continental Stitches.

5 Stitch handles according to graph, Overcasting edges as you stitch.

6 When background stitching is complete, Straight Stitch mouth using 6 strands embroidery floss. Straight Stitch whiskers using 3 strands embroidery floss.

7 Using white, Overcast top edges of body front and back between arrows. Using adjacent colors throughout, Overcast top edges of sides, and of head front and back between arrows.

8 Lay stitched head on stitched body with bottom and side edges even. Hot-glue head to body along upper edges of head and ears. Repeat with remaining head and body.

9 Using fern yarn throughout, Whipstitch front and back to sides along corners, stitching through all layers; Whipstitch tote bottom to front, back and sides.

10 Hot-glue ends of handles to wrong side of ears.

Bunny Head Front/Back
49 holes x 60 holes
Cut 2 from stiff

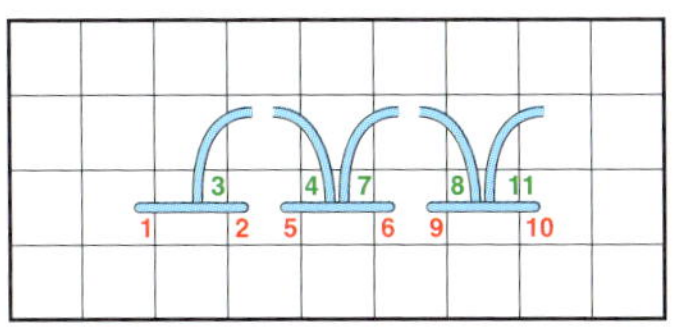

Turkey Loop Stitch

COLOR KEY

Yards	Plastic Canvas Yarn
3 (2.8m)	■ Black #00
11 (10.1m)	Pink #07
42 (38.4m)	Fern #23
10 (9.2m)	Baby blue #36
55 (50.3m)	White #41
5 (4.6m)	Purple #46
4 (3.7m)	Turquoise #54
19 (17.4m)	Watermelon #55
8 (7.4m)	Yellow #57
	Uncoded areas on head front/back are white #41 Continental Stitches
2 (1.9m)	○ White #41 Turkey Loop Stitch
	6-Strand Embroidery Floss
	/ Black #310 Straight Stitch

Color numbers given are for Uniek Needloft plastic canvas yarn and DMC 6-strand embroidery floss.

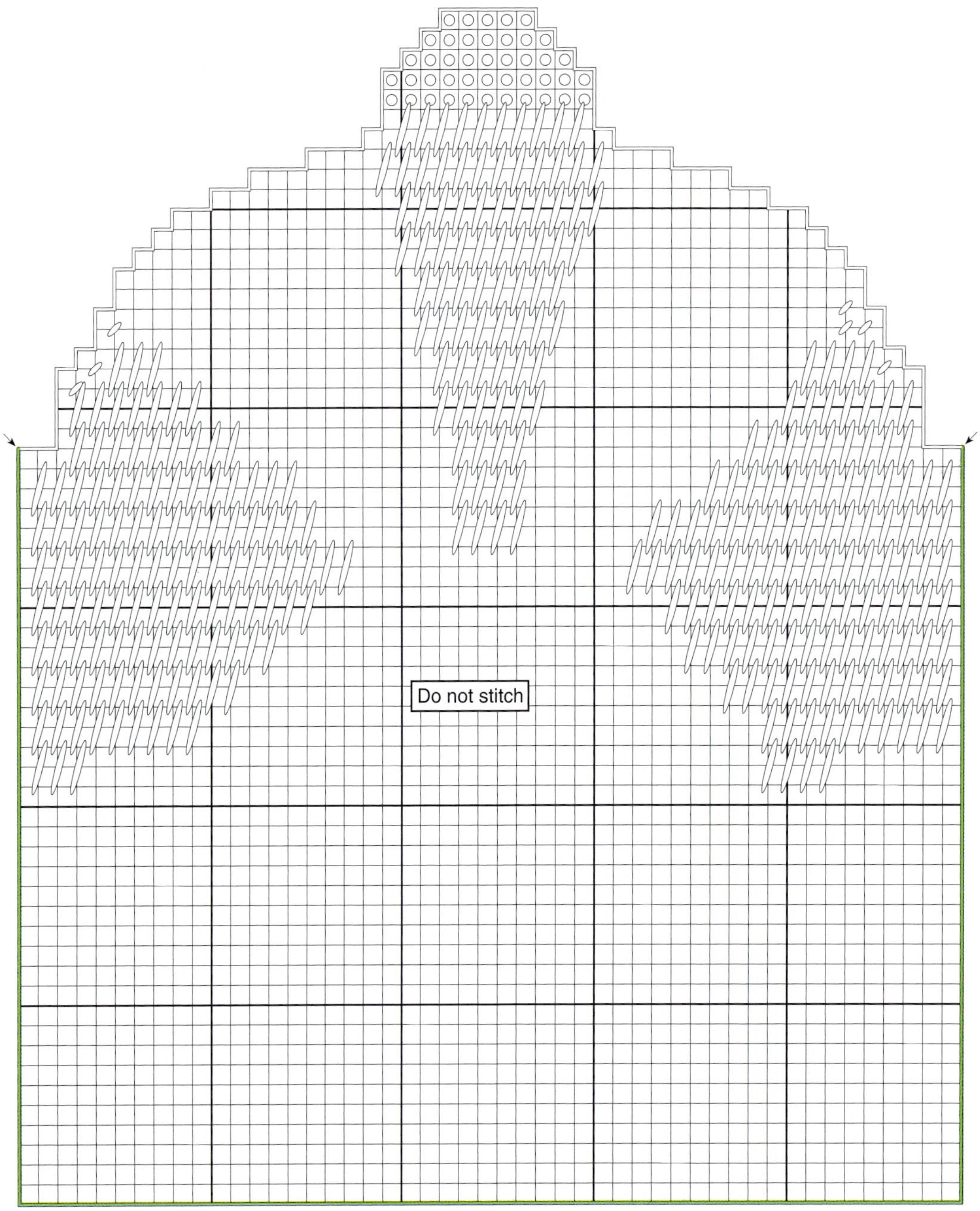

Bunny Body Front/Back
49 holes x 60 holes
Cut 2 from stiff

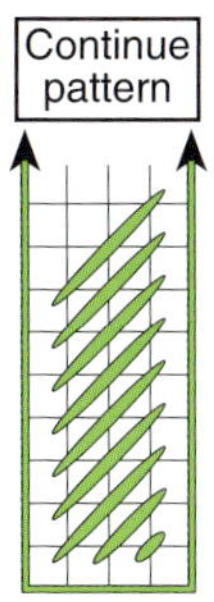

Bunny Handle
4 holes x 90 holes
Cut 2 from regular

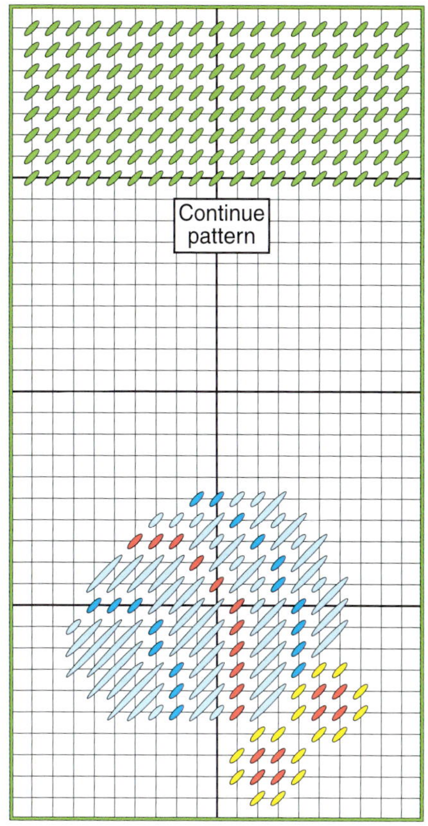

Bunny Side
20 holes x 38 holes
Cut 2 from regular

COLOR KEY	
Yards	**Plastic Canvas Yarn**
3 (2.8m)	■ Black #00
11 (10.1m)	□ Pink #07
42 (38.4m)	■ Fern #23
10 (9.2m)	□ Baby blue #36
55 (50.3m)	□ White #41
5 (4.6m)	■ Purple #46
4 (3.7m)	■ Turquoise #54
19 (17.4m)	■ Watermelon #55
8 (7.4m)	□ Yellow #57
	Uncoded areas on head front/back are white #41 Continental Stitches
2 (1.9m)	○ White #41 Turkey Loop Stitch
	6-Strand Embroidery Floss
	/ Black #310 Straight Stitch

Color numbers given are for Uniek Needloft plastic canvas yarn and DMC 6-strand embroidery floss.

Stained Glass Tulips

Size: 7 inches W x 8¼ inches H x 3¼ inches D (17.8cm x 21cm x 8.2cm) excluding handles
Skill Level: Beginner

Materials

- ❑ 7-count plastic canvas from Darice:
  1 sheet clear regular
  1 artist-size sheet (12-inch x 18-inch/ 30.5cm x 45.7cm) stiff
- ❑ Uniek Needloft plastic canvas yarn as listed in color key
- ❑ 2 yards (1.8m) ⅜-inch-wide (9mm) dusty rose ribbon
- ❑ #16 tapestry needle
- ❑ Hot-glue gun

Stitching Step by Step

1 *Cut plastic canvas according to graphs:* Cut two sides and two handles from regular, and two front/back pieces from stiff.

2 From regular plastic canvas, also cut one piece 45 holes x 20 holes for tote bottom; it will remain unstitched.

3 Stitch front, back, sides and handles according to graphs, Overcasting handles with matching yarn as you stitch.

4 Using black and white yarns according to graphs, Overcast top edges of sides, front and back.

5 Using white yarn throughout, Whipstitch front and back to sides along corners; Whipstitch tote bottom to front, back and sides.

6 Hot-glue ends of one handle to wrong side of tote front near corners. Repeat to attach handle to tote back.

7 Cut ribbon into four 18-inch (0.5m) pieces. Tie each in a bow around base of handle.

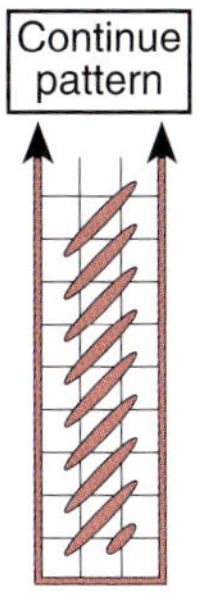

Stained Glass Tulips Handle
3 holes x 90 holes
Cut 2 from regular

Stained Glass Tulips Front/Back
45 holes x 54 holes
Cut 2 from stiff

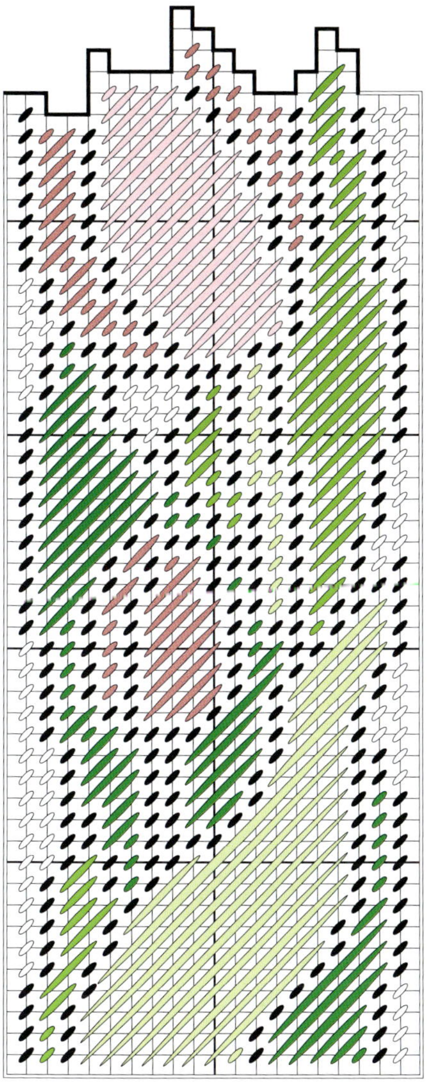

Stained Glass Tulips Side
20 holes x 50 holes
Cut 2 from regular

COLOR KEY

Yards	Plastic Canvas Yarn
35 (32m)	■ Black #00
16 (14.7m)	■ Lavender #05
12 (11m)	■ Pink #07
15 (13.8m)	■ Fern #23
15 (13.8m)	■ Moss #25
15 (13.8m)	■ Holly #27
12 (11m)	□ White #41
	⁄ Moss #25 Straight Stitch

Color numbers given are for Uniek Needloft plastic canvas yarn.

Kitty Cat

Size: 6¾ inches W x 12 inches H x 3 inches D (17.1cm x 30.5cm x 7.6cm) excluding handles
Skill Level: Beginner

Materials

- ❑ 7-count plastic canvas from Darice:
  ½ sheet clear regular
  1 artist-size sheet (12-inch x 18-inch/ 30.5cm x 45.7cm) stiff
- ❑ Uniek Needloft plastic canvas yarn as listed in color key
- ❑ DMC 6-strand embroidery floss as listed in color key
- ❑ 2 (½-inch/1.3cm) gold jingle bells
- ❑ Tapestry needles: #16, #18, #24

Stitching Step by Step

1 *Cut plastic canvas according to graphs:* Cut two sides from regular, and two front/back pieces from stiff.

2 From regular plastic canvas, also cut one piece 43 holes x 19 holes for tote bottom; it will remain unstitched.

3 Stitch front, back and sides according to graphs, filling in uncoded areas with pink Continental Stitches.

4 When background stitching is complete, using 6 strands embroidery floss throughout, Backstitch eyes, Straight Stitch mouth, Backstitch and Straight Stitch lettering, Straight Stitch paws, and work French Knots on mouth. Using 3 strands embroidery floss, Straight Stitch whiskers.

5 Using 3 strands embroidery floss, attach a jingle bell to front and another to back where indicated by red dots on graph.

6 Using adjacent colors on front and back, Whipstitch front and back to sides along corners, stitching through all layers and matching stitch direction. Using black, white and bittersweet yarns according to graph, Whipstitch tote bottom to front, back and sides. Using bittersweet along ears and adjacent colors elsewhere, Overcast all remaining unfinished edges.

COLOR KEY

Yards	Plastic Canvas Yarn
36 (33m)	■ Black #00
1 (1m)	■ Tangerine #11
22 (20.1m)	□ White #41
36 (33m)	■ Bittersweet #52
4 (3.7m)	■ Turquoise #54
5 (4.6m)	Uncoded areas are pink #07 Continental Stitches
	⁄ Pink #07 Overcast
	⁄ White #41 Straight Stitch
	6-Strand Embroidery Floss
2 (1.9m)	⁄ Black #310 (6-strand) Backstitch and Straight Stitch
	⁄ Black #310 (3-strand) Backstitch and Straight Stitch
	● Black #310 (6-strand) French Knot
	● Attach bell

Color numbers given are for Uniek Needloft plastic canvas yarn and DMC 6-strand embroidery floss.

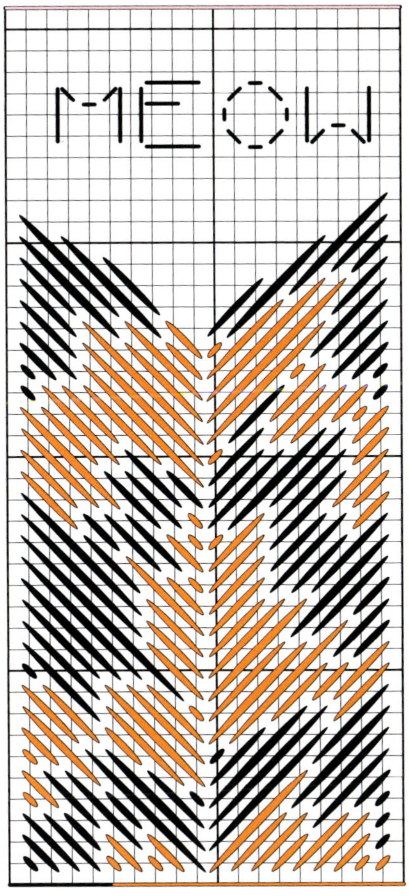

Kitty Cat Side
19 holes x 41 holes
Cut 2 from regular

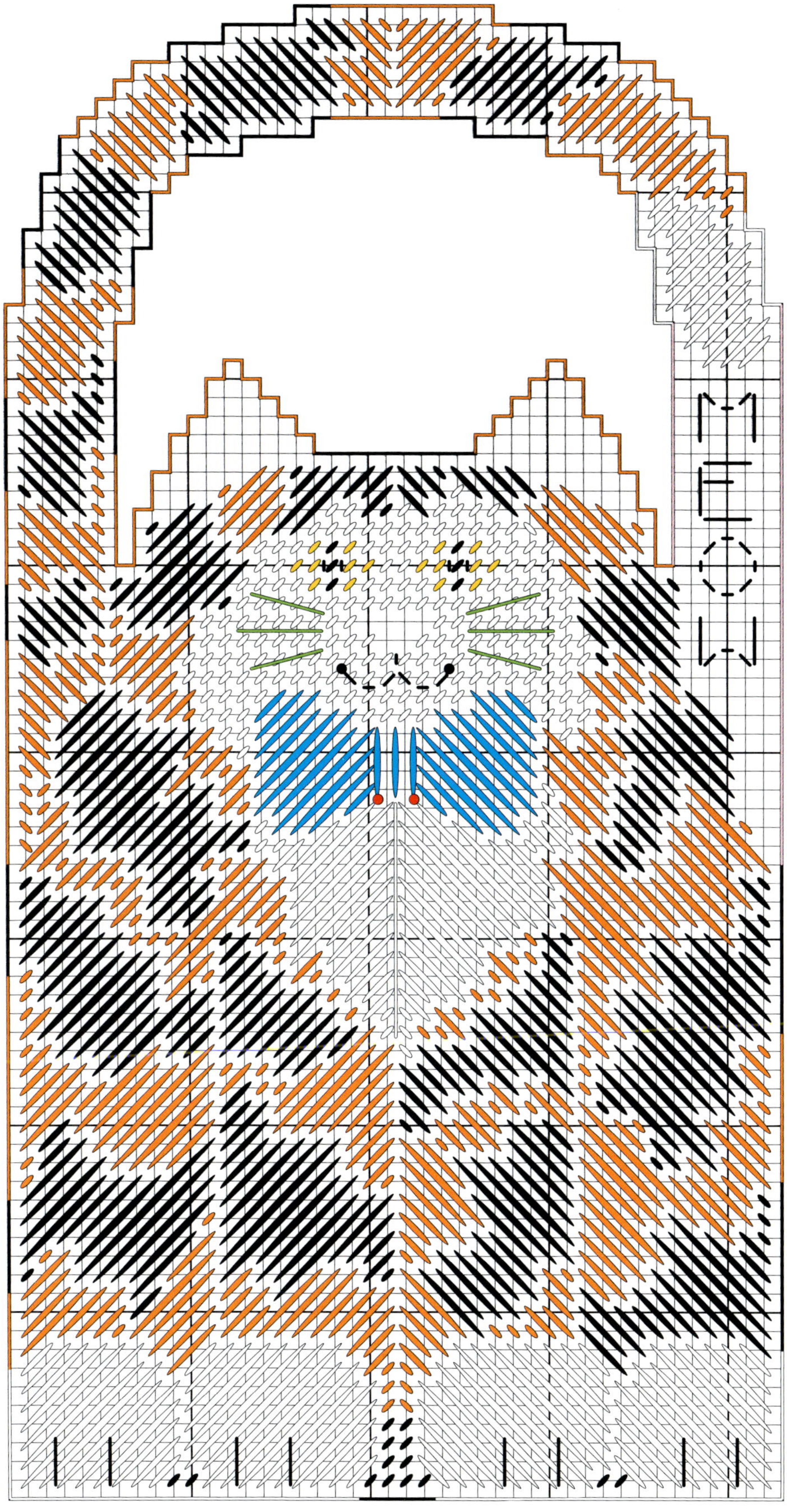

Kitty Cat Front/Back
43 holes x 80 holes
Cut 2 from stiff

Sunflower Birdhouse

Size: 6 inches W x 9½ inches H x 3⅛ inches D (15.2cm x 24.1cm x 7.9cm) excluding handles
Skill Level: Beginner

Materials

- ❑ 7-count plastic canvas from Darice:
  - ½ sheet clear regular
  - 1 sheet stiff
- ❑ Uniek Needloft plastic canvas yarn as listed in color key
- ❑ 2 (18-inch/45.7cm) brown paper-wrapped 18-gauge wire stems
- ❑ #16 tapestry needle
- ❑ Hot-glue gun

Stitching Step by Step

1 *Cut plastic canvas according to graphs:* Cut two sides from regular, and two front/back pieces and two roof pieces from stiff.

2 From regular plastic canvas, also cut one piece 38 holes x 20 holes for tote bottom; it will remain unstitched.

3 Stitch front, back, sides and roofs according to graphs, leaving unstitched areas along diagonal edges of front and back as noted, and filling in remaining uncoded area in center of flower with brown Continental Stitches.

4 Using royal yarn throughout, Overcast roofs and top edges of front, back and sides. Whipstitch front and back to sides along corners; Whipstitch tote bottom to front, back and sides.

5 Hot-glue roofs to front and back of tote over unstitched areas.

6 Hot-glue ends of one wire stem to wrong side of tote front to form handle; repeat to attach handle to back of tote.

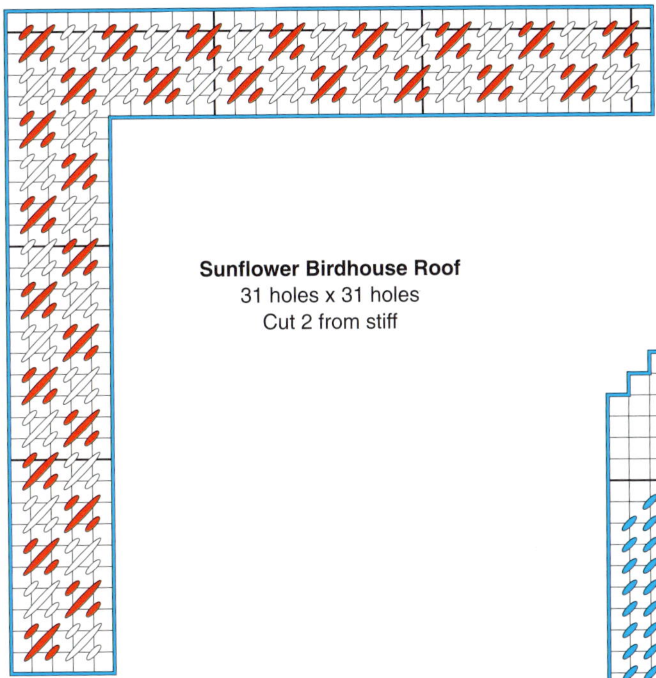

Sunflower Birdhouse Roof
31 holes x 31 holes
Cut 2 from stiff

Sunflower Birdhouse Front/Back
38 holes x 62 holes
Cut 2 from stiff

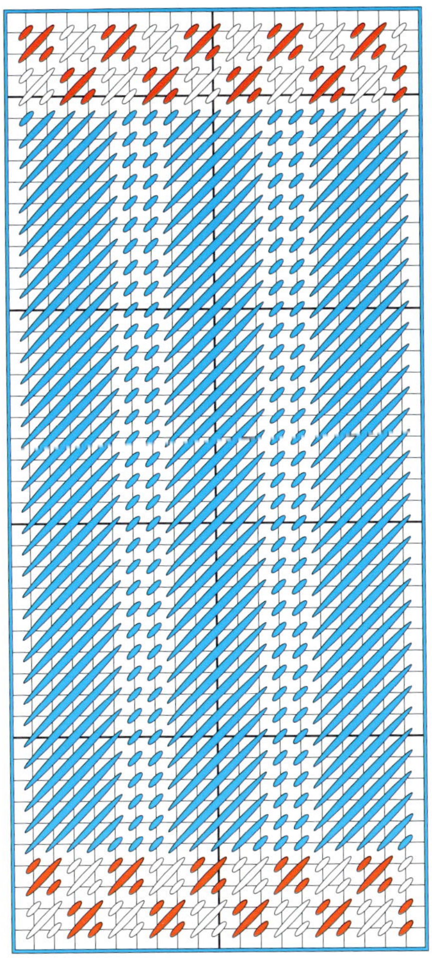

Sunflower Birdhouse Side
20 holes x 44 holes
Cut 2 from regular

COLOR KEY

Yards	Plastic Canvas Yarn
9 (8.3m)	Red #01
8 (7.4m)	Gold #17
5 (4.6m)	Moss #25
50 (45.7m)	Royal #32
10 (9.2m)	White #41
9 (8.3m)	Yellow #57
5 (4.6m)	Uncoded area in flower center is brown #15 Continental Stitches

Color numbers given are for Uniek Needloft plastic canvas yarn.

Watering Can

Size: 8¾ inches W x 7⅝ inches H x 3¼ inches D (22.2cm x 19.4cm x 8.3cm) excluding handles
Skill Level: Beginner

Materials

- ❑ 7-count plastic canvas from Darice:
  - ½ sheet clear regular
  - 1 artist-size sheet (12-inch x 18-inch/ 30.5cm x 45.7cm) stiff
- ❑ Uniek Needloft plastic canvas yarn as listed in color key
- ❑ Flat white 4-hole buttons:
  - 4 (⅝-inch/1.6cm)
  - 4 (⅜-inch/1cm)
- ❑ Tapestry needles: #16, #22
- ❑ Hot-glue gun

Stitching Step by Step

1 *Cut plastic canvas according to graphs:* Cut two sides and one handle from regular, and two front/ back pieces from stiff.

2 From regular plastic canvas, also cut one piece 57 holes x 21 holes for tote bottom; it will remain unstitched.

3 Stitch front, back, sides and handles according to graphs.

4 When background stitching is complete, work Straight Stitches on watering can using fern, and French Knots using purple.

5 Using 1 ply separated from a length of watermelon yarn, attach a large button to the large watermelon flower, working a cross stitch through the holes in the button; repeat to attach a small button to the small watermelon flower. In the same manner, use 1 ply separated from a length of watermelon yarn to attach remaining large button to large purple flower, and small button to small purple flower.

6 Using adjacent colors throughout, Overcast top edges of front, back and sides, and Overcast handle.

7 Using white yarn, Whipstitch front and back to sides along corners; using adjacent colors, Whipstitch tote bottom to front, back and sides.

8 Center and hot-glue ends of handle to wrong side of tote front and back.

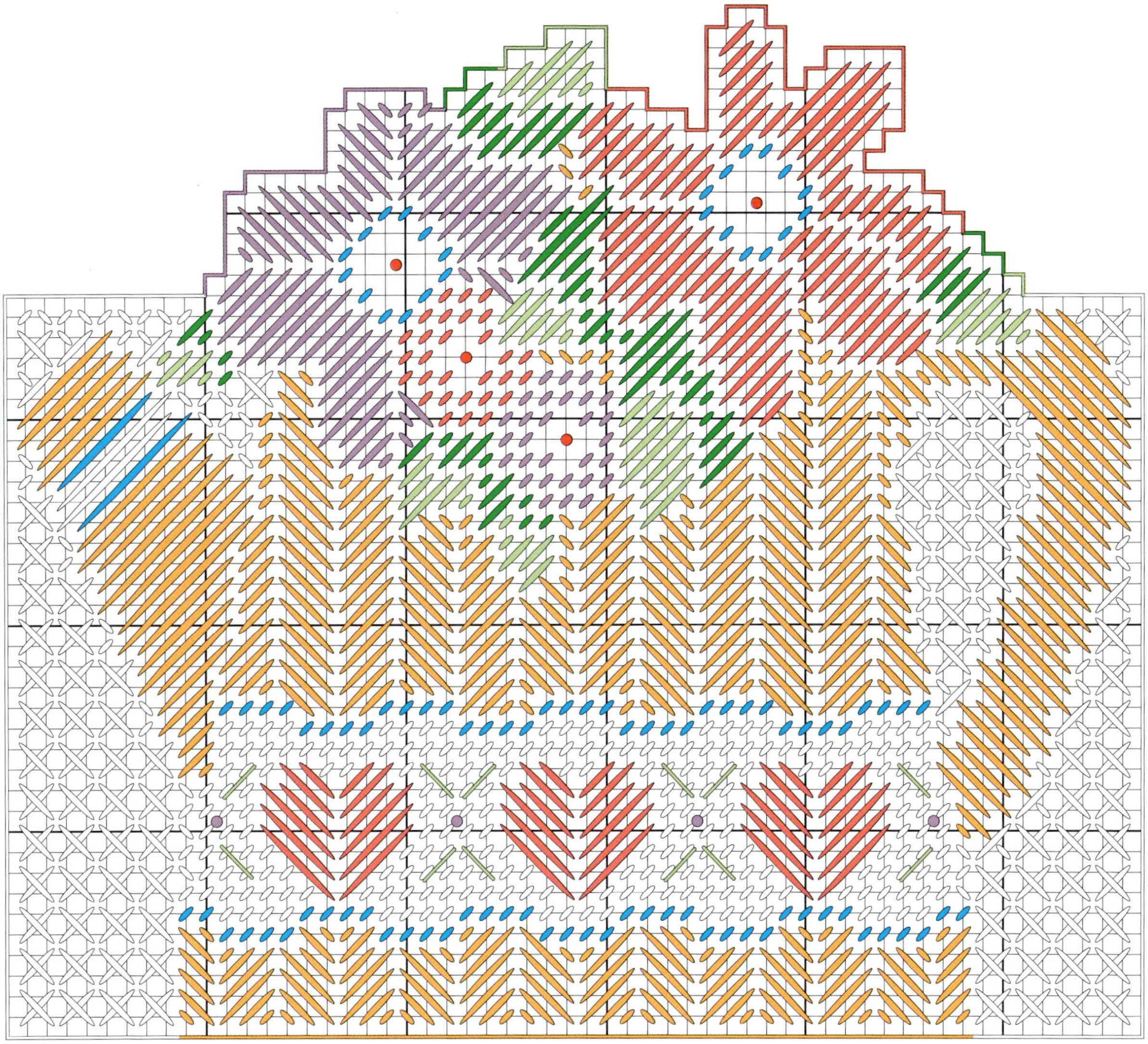

Watering Can Front/Back
57 holes x 50 holes
Cut 2 from stiff

COLOR KEY

Yards	Plastic Canvas Yarn
42 (38.4m)	Tangerine #11
6 (5.5m)	Fern #23
6 (5.5m)	Christmas green #28
42 (38.4m)	White #41
8 (7.4m)	Purple #46
6 (5.5m)	Turquoise #54
8 (7.4m)	Watermelon #55
	Fern #23 Straight Stitch
	Purple #46 French Knot
	Attach button

Color numbers given are for Uniek Needloft plastic canvas yarn.

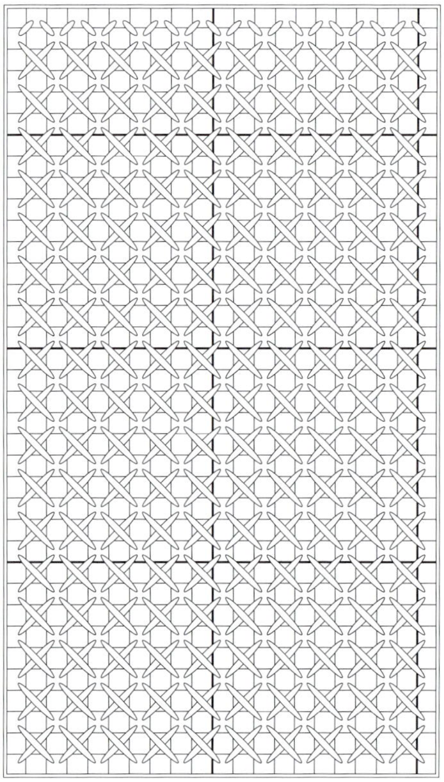

Watering Can Side
21 holes x 36 holes
Cut 2 from regular

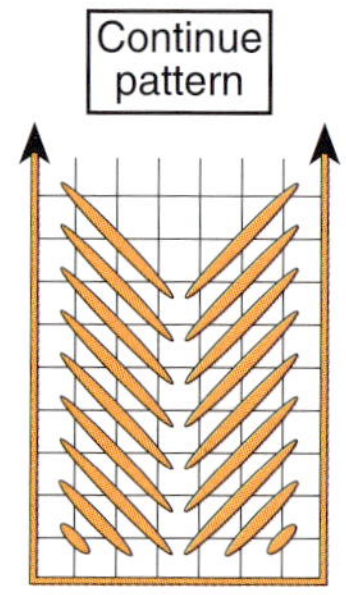

Watering Can Handle
7 holes x 70 holes
Cut 1 from regular

COLOR KEY	
Yards	**Plastic Canvas Yarn**
42 (38.4m)	Tangerine #11
6 (5.5m)	Fern #23
6 (5.5m)	Christmas green #28
42 (38.4m)	White #41
8 (7.4m)	Purple #46
6 (5.5m)	Turquoise #54
8 (7.4m)	Watermelon #55
	Fern #23 Straight Stitch
	Purple #46 French Knot
	Attach button

Color numbers given are for Uniek Needloft plastic canvas yarn.

Autumn Apples

Size: 6⅝ inches W x 8⅝ inches H x 3 inches D (16.8cm x 21.9cm x 7.6cm) excluding handles
Skill Level: Beginner

Materials

- ❑ 7-count plastic canvas from Darice:
  - ½ sheet clear regular
  - 1 sheet stiff
- ❑ Uniek Needloft plastic canvas yarn as listed in color key
- ❑ DMC 6-strand embroidery floss as listed in color key
- ❑ 40 inches (1m) ¼-inch-diameter (7mm) natural rope
- ❑ Tapestry needles: #16, #20
- ❑ Hot-glue gun

Stitching Step by Step

1 *Cut plastic canvas according to graphs:* Cut two sides from regular, and two front/back pieces from stiff.

2 From regular plastic canvas, also cut one piece 43 holes x 19 holes for tote bottom; it will remain unstitched.

3 Stitch front, back and sides according to graphs, filling in uncoded areas with white Continental Stitches.

4 When background stitching is complete, Straight Stitch lettering on front and back using royal blue embroidery floss. Work Lazy Daisy Stitch seeds on cut apple using cinnamon yarn.

5 Using adjacent colors throughout, Overcast top edges of front, back and sides, and Overcast openings in front and back.

6 Using sandstone yarn throughout, Whipstitch front and back to sides along corners; Whipstitch tote bottom to front, back and sides.

7 *Handles:* Cut rope in half. Thread ends of one piece from front to back through holes in tote front. Tie knots in ends; hot-glue knots inside tote. Repeat to attach handle to back of tote.

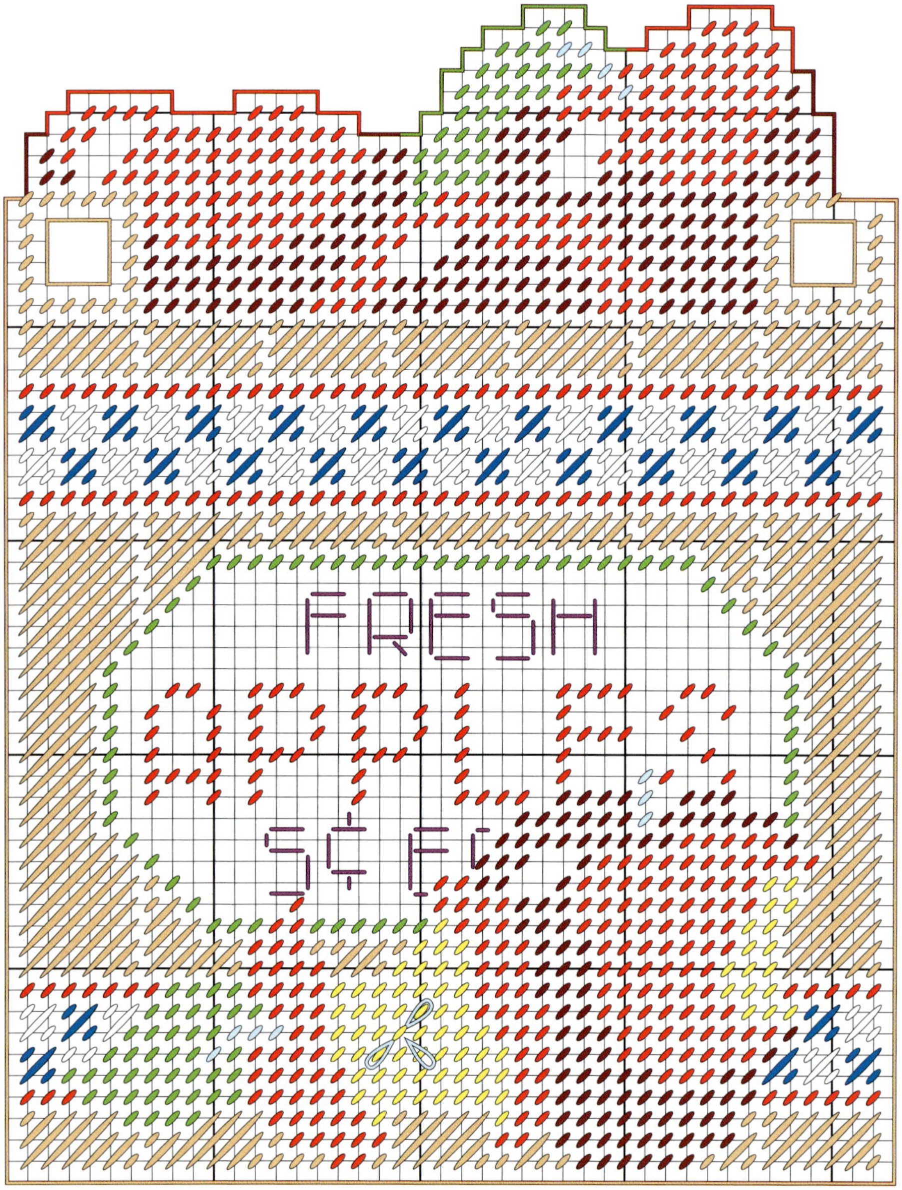

Autumn Apples Front/Back
43 holes x 55 holes
Cut 2 from stiff

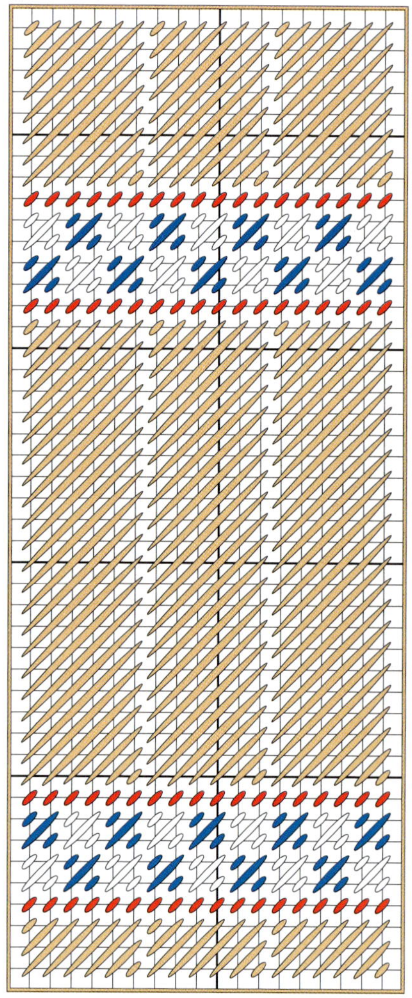

Autumn Apples Side
19 holes x 46 holes
Cut 2 from regular

COLOR KEY

Yards	Plastic Canvas Yarn
19 (17.4m)	Red #01
13 (11.9m)	Burgundy #03
1 (1m)	Cinnamon #14
36 (33m)	Sandstone #16
6 (5.5m)	Moss #25
4 (3.7m)	Eggshell #39
27 (24.7m)	White #41
9 (8.3m)	Dark royal #48
	Uncoded areas are white #41 Continental Stitches
	Cinnamon #14 Lazy Daisy Stitch
	6-Strand Embroidery Floss
2 (1.8m)	Royal blue #797 Backstitch and Straight Stitch

Color numbers given are for Uniek Needloft plastic canvas yarn and DMC 6-strand embroidery floss.

Goofy Ghost

Size: 6¼ inches W x 8⅞ inches H x 3 inches D (15.9cm x 22.5cm x 7.6cm) excluding handles
Skill Level: Beginner

Materials

- ❑ 7-count plastic canvas from Darice:
  - ½ sheet clear regular
  - 1 sheet stiff
- ❑ Uniek Needloft plastic canvas yarn as listed in color key
- ❑ DMC 6-strand embroidery floss as listed in color key
- ❑ 4 (12mm) oval movable eyes
- ❑ 2 (18-inch/45.7cm) brown paper-wrapped 18-gauge wire stems
- ❑ Natural raffia
- ❑ Tapestry needles: #16, #18
- ❑ Hot-glue gun

Stitching Step by Step

1 *Cut plastic canvas according to graphs:* Cut two sides and four hands from regular, and two front/back pieces from stiff.

2 From regular plastic canvas, also cut one piece 40 holes x 19 holes for tote bottom; it will remain unstitched.

3 Stitch front, back, sides and hands according to graphs, filling in uncoded areas with white Continental Stitches.

4 When background stitching is complete, using very dark green embroidery floss, Backstitch and Straight Stitch pumpkin tendrils, leaf veins and grass; using black embroidery floss, Backstitch and Straight Stitch all other details.

5 Using white yarn throughout, Overcast curved edges of hands between arrows; Overcast top edges of front and back. Position straight edges of hands along side edges of front and back between arrows; Whipstitch straight edges of hands to front and back. Bending hands slightly, tack front edges of hands to front and back where indicated by red stars on front/back graph.

6 Using fern and forest yarns according to graphs, Whipstitch front and back to sides along corners. Using fern, Whipstitch tote bottom to front, back and sides. Using forest, Overcast top edges of sides.

7 *Handles:* Beginning 3½ inches (8.9cm) from one end, wrap one wire stem around a pencil five times to form loops. Slide wire off pencil. Hot-glue one end of wire inside ghost's hand on tote front. Stretch wire to form handle; hot-glue other end inside other hand. Repeat to attach handle to back of tote.

8 Tie raffia in a bow around each handle. Hot-glue movable eyes to ghost.

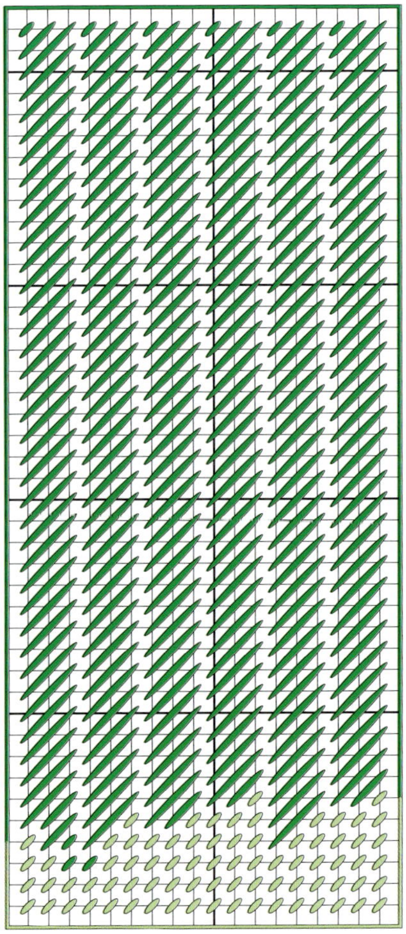

Goofy Ghost Side
19 holes x 43 holes
Cut 2 from regular;
stitch 1 in mirror image

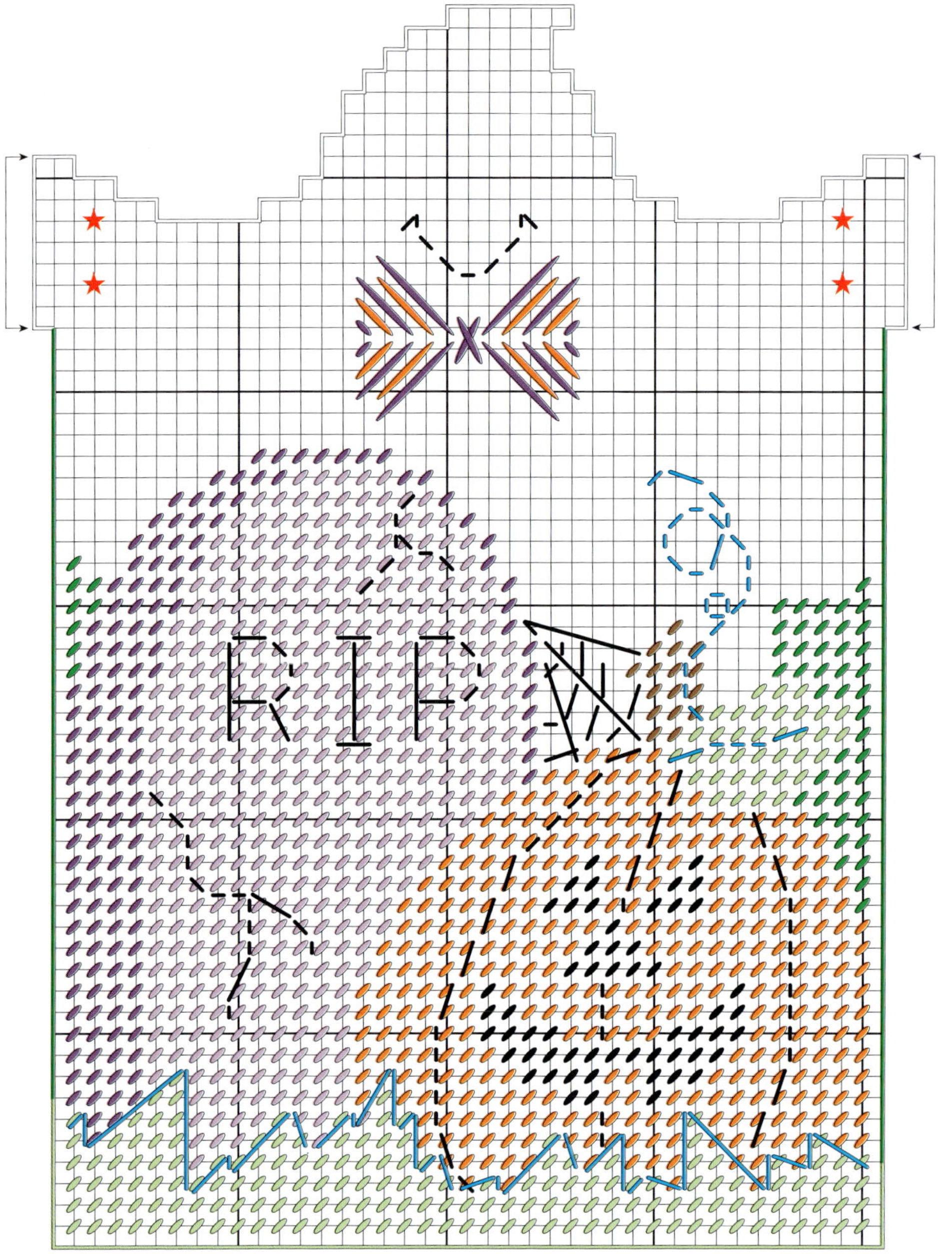

Goofy Ghost Front/Back
42 holes x 58 holes
Cut 2 from stiff

COLOR KEY

Yards	Plastic Canvas Yarn
3 (2.8m)	■ Black #00
1 (1m)	■ Cinnamon #14
14 (12.8m)	■ Fern #23
23 (21.1m)	■ Forest #29
16 (14.7m)	■ Lilac #45
10 (9.2m)	■ Bittersweet #52
8 (7.4m)	■ Bright purple #64
33 (30.2m)	Uncoded areas are white #41 Continental Stitches
	⁄ White #41 Overcast
	6-Strand Embroidery Floss
7 (6.5m)	⁄ Black #310 Backstitch and Straight Stitch
5 (4.6m)	⁄ Very dark green #986 Backstitch and Straight Stitch
	★ Attach hands

Color numbers given are for Uniek Needloft plastic canvas yarn and DMC 6-strand embroidery floss.

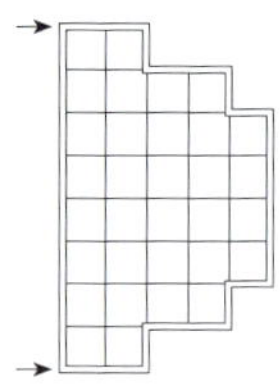

Goofy Ghost Hand
5 holes x 8 holes
Cut 4, reverse 2, from regular

Winter Snowman

Size: 6⅜ inches W x 11¼ inches H x 3 inches D (16.2cm x 28.6cm x 7.6cm) excluding handles
Skill Level: Beginner

Materials

- ❑ 7-count plastic canvas from Darice:
  - ½ sheet clear regular
  - 1 artist-size sheet (12-inch x 18-inch/ 30.5cm x 45.7cm) stiff
- ❑ Uniek Needloft plastic canvas yarn as listed in color key
- ❑ DMC 6-strand embroidery floss as listed in color key
- ❑ Madeira GlissenGloss 4mm metallic braid ribbon as listed in color key
- ❑ Tapestry needles: #16, #20
- ❑ Hot-glue gun

Stitching Step by Step

1 *Cut plastic canvas according to graphs:* Cut two sides and four mittens from regular, and two front/back pieces from stiff.

2 From regular plastic canvas, also cut one piece 41 holes x 19 holes for tote bottom; it will remain unstitched.

3 Stitch front, back, sides and mittens according to graphs, reversing two mittens before stitching, and leaving uncoded areas and red lines on front and back unstitched.

4 When background stitching is complete, Straight Stitch mouth using black embroidery floss. Using 2 plies separated from a length of black yarn, work French Knots for eyes.

5 Overcast rounded edges of mittens between arrows using holly yarn according to graph. Positioning unfinished edges of one pair of mittens along rows indicated by red lines on front/back graph, Whipstitch mittens to tote front using bright purple yarn. Repeat to attach remaining mittens to tote back.

6 Using white and bright purple yarns according to graph, Overcast top edges of snowman and hat on front and back.

7 Using royal yarn throughout, Whipstitch front and back to sides along corners; Whipstitch tote bottom to front, back and sides. Overcast remaining unfinished edges.

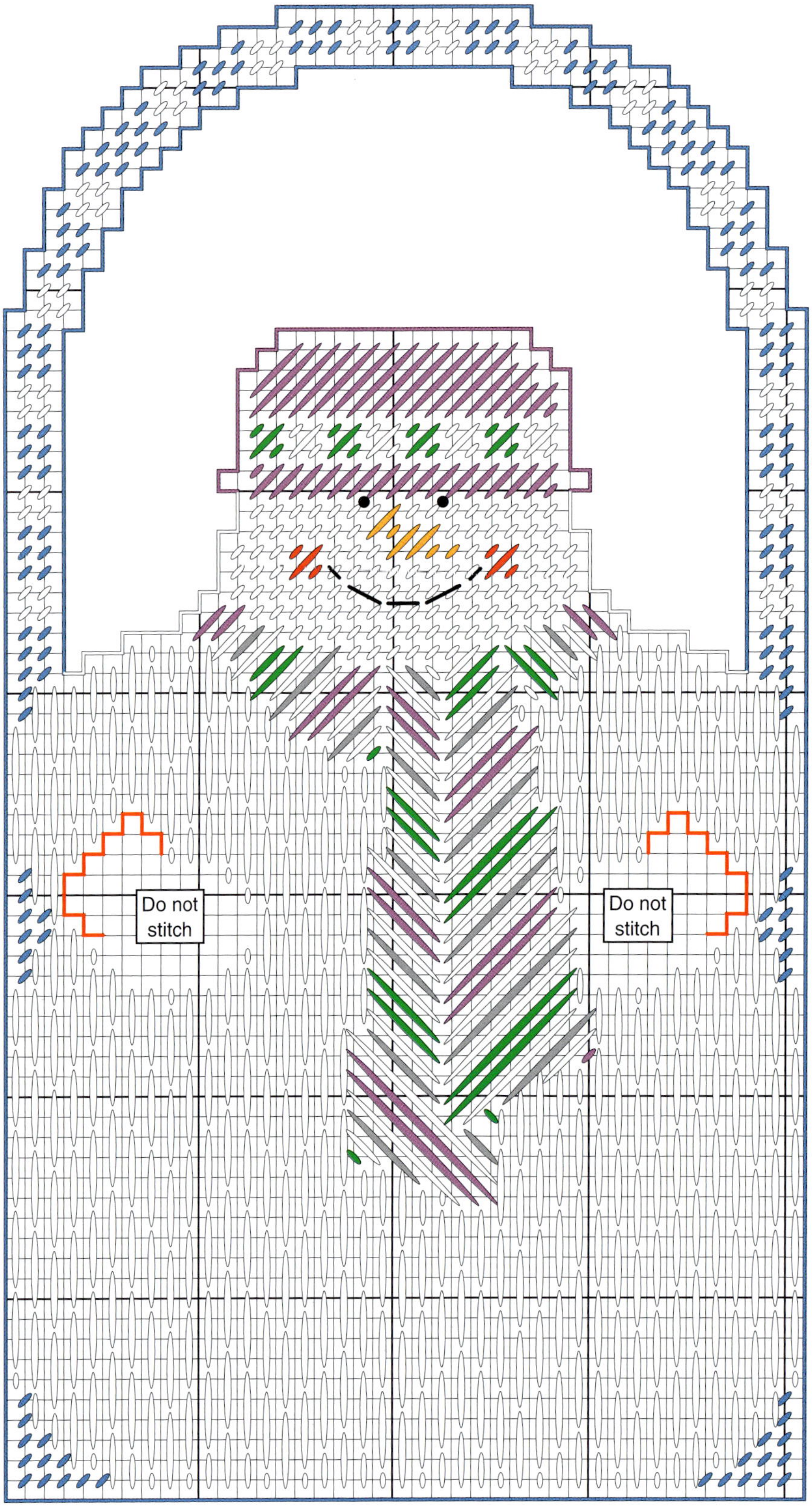

Winter Snowman Front/Back
41 holes x 74 holes
Cut 2 from stiff

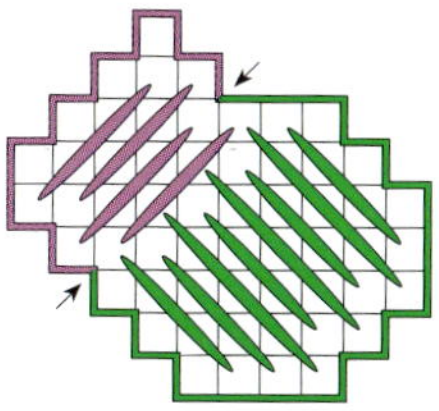

Winter Snowman Mitten
10 holes x 9 holes
Cut 4 from regular,
reverse 2 before stitching

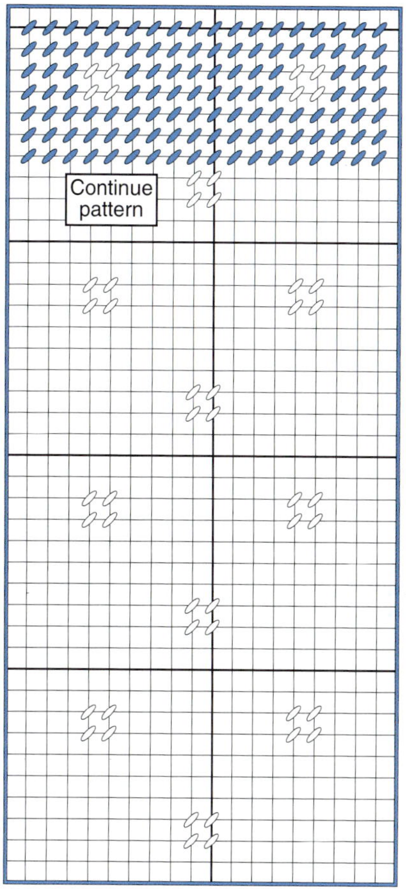

Winter Snowman Side
19 holes x 41 holes
Cut 2 from regular

COLOR KEY

Yards	Plastic Canvas Yarn
6 (5.5m)	Holly #27
50 (45.7m)	Royal #32
50 (45.7m)	White #41
1 (1m)	Watermelon #55
1 (1m)	Bright orange #58
9 (8.3m)	Bright purple #64
1 (1m)	● Black #00 (2-ply) French Knot
	Metallic Braid Ribbon
15 (13.8m)	Silver #02 (4mm)
	6-Strand Embroidery Floss
1 (1m)	/ Black #310 Straight Stitch

Color numbers given are for Uniek Needloft plastic canvas yarn, Madeira GlissenGloss metallic braid ribbon and DMC 6-strand embroidery floss.

Li'l Angel

Size: 5¼ inches W x 7¼ inches H x 3 inches D (13.3cm x 18.4cm x 7.6cm) excluding handles
Skill Level: Beginner

Materials

- ❑ 7-count plastic canvas from Darice:
  - ½ sheet clear regular
  - 1 sheet stiff
- ❑ Uniek Needloft plastic canvas yarn as listed in color key
- ❑ DMC 6-strand embroidery floss as listed in color key
- ❑ Madeira GlissenGloss 2mm and 4mm metallic braid ribbon as listed in color key
- ❑ Tapestry needles: #16, #18
- ❑ Hot-glue gun

Stitching Step by Step

1 *Cut plastic canvas according to graphs:* Cut two sides and two arms from regular, and two front/back pieces from stiff.

2 From regular plastic canvas, also cut two pieces 81 holes x 2 holes for handles, and one piece 37 holes x 17 holes for tote bottom; tote bottom will remain unstitched.

3 Stitch front, back, arms and sides according to graphs, leaving red lines on front and back unstitched, and filling in uncoded areas with moss Continental Stitches. Fill in handles with white Continental Stitches.

4 When background stitching is complete, Backstitch mouth using red embroidery floss. Backstitch stripes on gown using 2mm dark gold metallic braid ribbon.

5 Using 2 plies separated from lengths of yarn, work French Knots according to graph, using cinnamon for eyes, and white and watermelon on gown hem and sleeve cuffs.

6 Overcast top and bottom edges of arms between arrows using white and light peach yarns and dark gold 4mm metallic braid ribbon according to graph. Positioning unfinished edges of one set of arms along rows indicated by red lines on front/back graph, Whipstitch arms to front. Repeat to attach remaining arms to back.

7 Using cinnamon yarn, Overcast hair on front and back. Using dark gold 4mm metallic braid ribbon throughout, Overcast top edges of sides, front and back, including halos; Overcast handles.

8 Using opal white 4mm metallic braid ribbon, Whipstitch front and back to sides along corners. Using white yarn, Whipstitch tote bottom to front, back and sides.

9 Hot-glue ends of handles to wrong sides of front and back near corners.

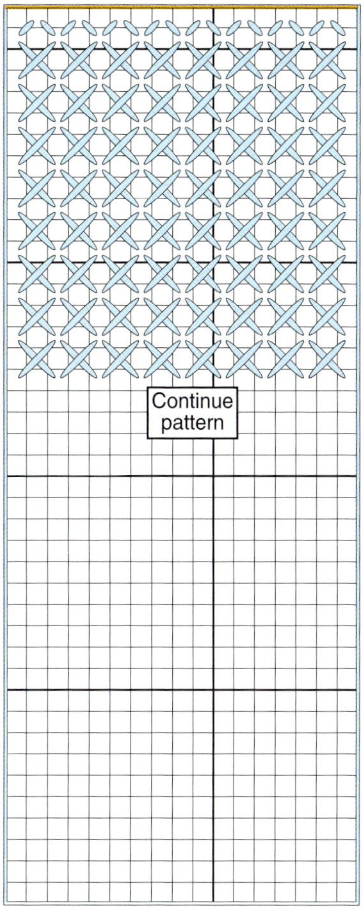

Li'l Angel Side
17 holes x 42 holes
Cut 2 from regular

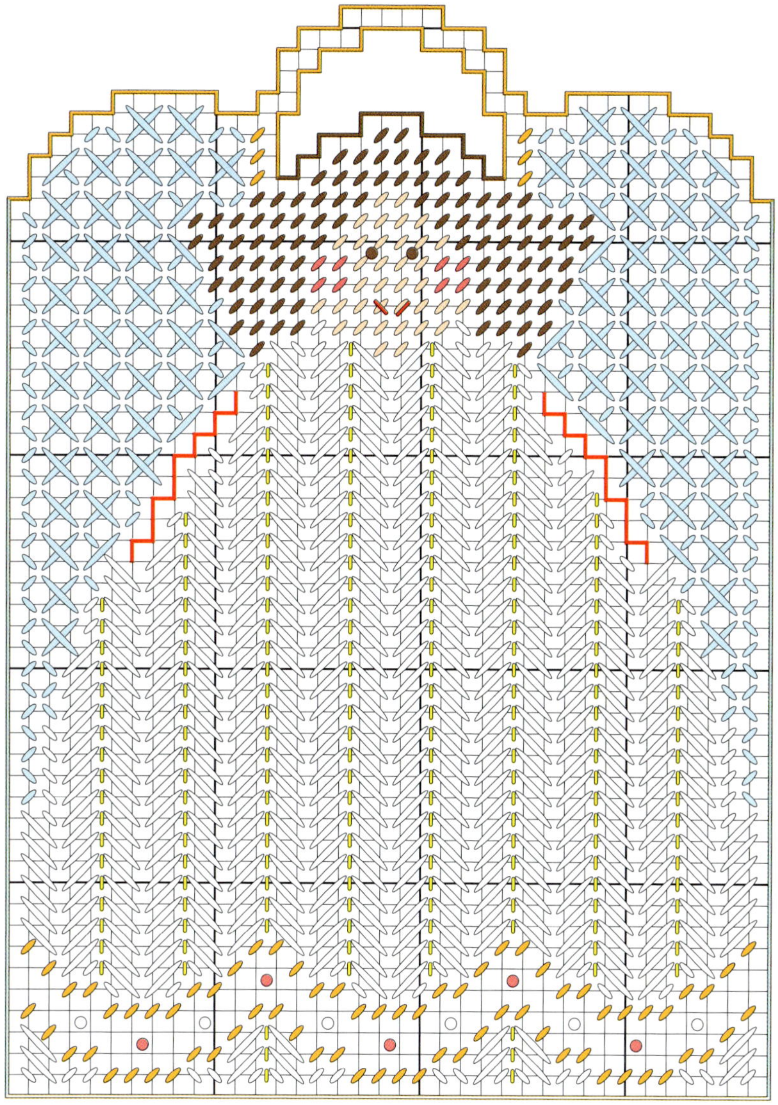

Li'l Angel Front/Back
37 holes x 51 holes
Cut 2 from stiff

COLOR KEY

Yards	Plastic Canvas Yarn
4 (3.7m)	■ Cinnamon #14
40 (36.6m)	□ White #41
2 (1.9m)	■ Watermelon #55
3 (2.8m)	■ Light peach #56
3 (2.8m)	Uncoded areas are moss #25 Continental Stitches
	● Cinnamon #14 (2-ply) French Knot
	○ White #41 (2-ply) French Knot
	● Watermelon #55 (2-ply) French Knot
	Metallic Braid Ribbon
35 (32m)	□ Opal white #07 (4mm)
13 (11.9m)	■ Dark gold #01 (4mm)
7 (6.5m)	⁄ Dark gold #01 (2mm) Backstitch
	6-Strand Embroidery Floss
2 (1.9m)	⁄ Red #321 Backstitch

Color numbers given are for Uniek Needloft plastic canvas yarn, Madeira GlissenGloss metallic braid ribbon and DMC 6-strand embroidery floss.

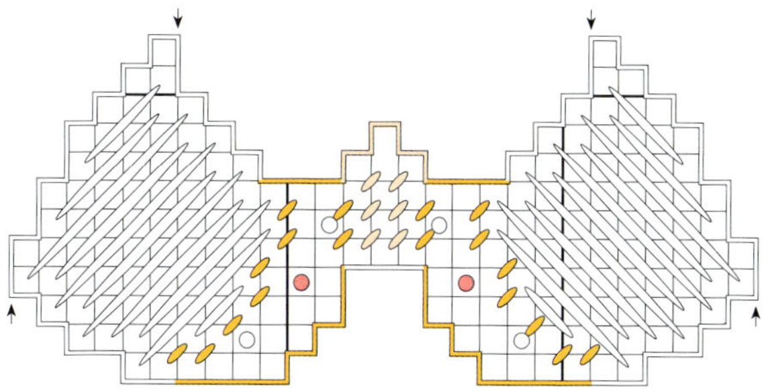

Li'l Angel Arms
27 holes x 12 holes
Cut 2 from regular

Candy Cane Bear

Size: 6½ inches W x 7¼ inches H x 3 inches D (16.5cm x 18.4cm x 7.6cm) excluding handles
Skill Level: Beginner

Materials

- ❑ 7-count plastic canvas from Darice:
  - ½ sheet clear regular
  - 1 sheet stiff
- ❑ 2 (6-inch/15.2cm) plastic canvas radial circles from Darice
- ❑ Uniek Needloft plastic canvas yarn as listed in color key
- ❑ DMC 6-strand embroidery floss: 12 inches (30.5cm) bright red #666, and as listed in color key
- ❑ 2 (½-inch/1.3cm) silver jingle bells
- ❑ Tapestry needles: #16, #18
- ❑ Hot-glue gun

Stitching Step by Step

1 *Cut plastic canvas according to graphs:* Cut two sides from regular; two front/back pieces from stiff; and two handles from plastic canvas circles.

2 From regular plastic canvas, also cut one piece 42 holes x 19 holes for tote bottom; it will remain unstitched.

3 Stitch front, back, sides and handles according to graphs, filling in uncoded areas with camel Continental Stitches, and referring to stitch diagrams to work Turkey Loop Stitches where indicated for scarf fringe. Clip loops; trim ends even.

4 When background stitching is complete, Backstitch and Straight Stitch details using black embroidery floss.

5 Using 3 strands bright red embroidery floss, attach a jingle bell to tip of hat on front and back where indicated by gold dot on graph.

6 Overcast top edges of front and back according to graph; Overcast handles using red and white according to graph.

7 Using moss throughout, Whipstitch front and back to sides along corners. Whipstitch tote bottom to front, back and sides. Overcast top edges of sides.

8 Center and hot-glue ends of handles to wrong sides of tote front and back.

Candy Cane Bear Front/Back
42 holes x 47 holes
Cut 2 from stiff

COLOR KEY	
Yards	**Plastic Canvas Yarn**
1 (1m)	■ Black #00
17 (15.6m)	■ Red #01
7 (6.5m)	■ Burgundy #03
2 (1.9m)	■ Pink #07
4 (3.7m)	■ Cinnamon #14
30 (27.5m)	■ Moss #25
7 (6.5m)	■ Holly #27
4 (3.7m)	■ Eggshell #39
18 (16.5m)	□ White #41
20 (18.3m)	Uncoded areas are camel #43 Continental Stitches
	○ White #41 Turkey Loop Stitch
	6-Strand Embroidery Floss
2 (1.9m)	⁄ Black #310 Backstitch and Straight Stitch
	● Attach bell

Color numbers given are for Uniek Needloft plastic canvas yarn and DMC 6-strand embroidery floss.

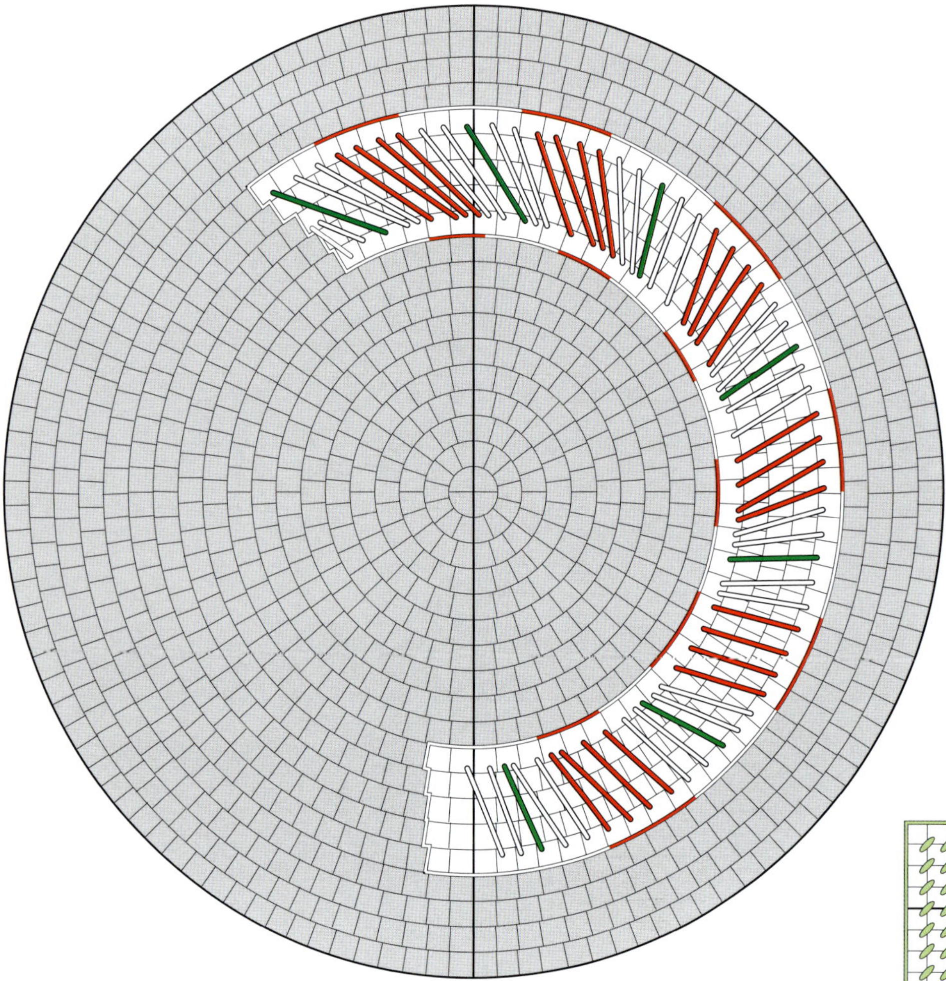

Candy Cane Bear Handle
Cut 2 from 6-inch plastic canvas radial circles

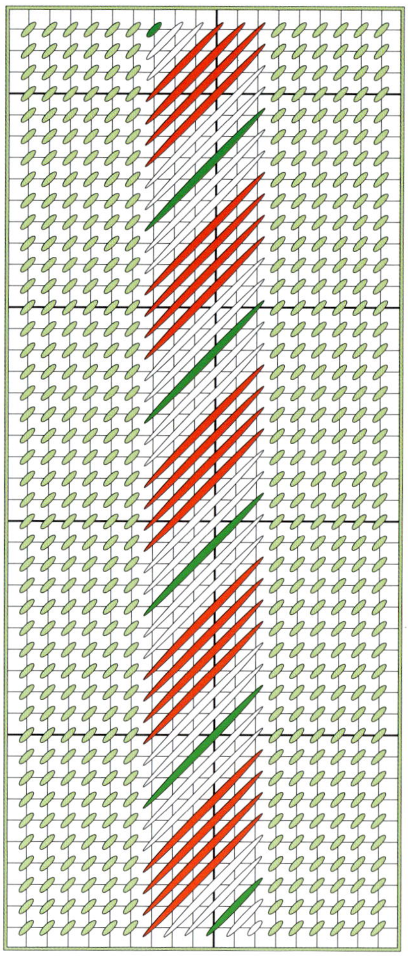

Candy Cane Bear Side
19 holes x 44 holes
Cut 2 from regular

COLOR KEY	
Yards	**Plastic Canvas Yarn**
1 (1m)	■ Black #00
17 (15.6m)	■ Red #01
7 (6.5m)	■ Burgundy #03
2 (1.9m)	■ Pink #07
4 (3.7m)	■ Cinnamon #14
30 (27.5m)	■ Moss #25
7 (6.5m)	■ Holly #27
4 (3.7m)	■ Eggshell #39
18 (16.5m)	□ White #41
20 (18.3m)	Uncoded areas are camel #43 Continental Stitches
	○ White #41 Turkey Loop Stitch
	6-Strand Embroidery Floss
2 (1.9m)	╱ Black #310 Backstitch and Straight Stitch
	● Attach bell

Color numbers given are for Uniek Needloft plastic canvas yarn and DMC 6-strand embroidery floss.

Santa

Size: 7⅜ inches W x 9¾ inches H x 3 inches D (18.7cm x 24.8cm x 7.6cm) excluding handles
Skill Level: Beginner

Materials

- ❑ 7-count plastic canvas from Darice:
  1 sheet stiff
- ❑ 2 (5-inch/12.7cm) plastic canvas stars from Darice
- ❑ Uniek Needloft plastic canvas yarn as listed in color key
- ❑ Madeira GlissenGloss 4mm metallic braid ribbon as listed in color key
- ❑ DMC 6-strand embroidery floss as listed in color key
- ❑ 2 (¾-inch/1.9cm) silver jingle bells
- ❑ Tapestry needles: #16, #22
- ❑ Hot-glue gun

Stitching Step by Step

1 *Cut plastic canvas according to graphs:* Cut two sides from regular; two front/back pieces from stiff; and two stars from plastic canvas stars.

2 From regular plastic canvas, also cut one piece 48 holes x 19 holes for tote bottom; it will remain unstitched.

3 Stitch front, back and sides according to graphs, filling in uncoded areas with light peach Continental Stitches, and working vertical Straight Stitches of mouth and nose with *doubled* strands of yarn.

4 Stitch stars according to graph, Overcasting edges as you stitch.

5 When background stitching is complete, Straight Stitch nose and hat brim using very dark gray embroidery floss.

6 Using burgundy yarn throughout, Whipstitch front and back to sides along corners; Whipstitch tote bottom to front, back and sides. Overcast all remaining unfinished edges.

7 Using white yarn, stitch jingle bell to tip of Santa's hat on tote front and back where indicated by red dot on graph. Hot-glue star to hat brim on front and back.

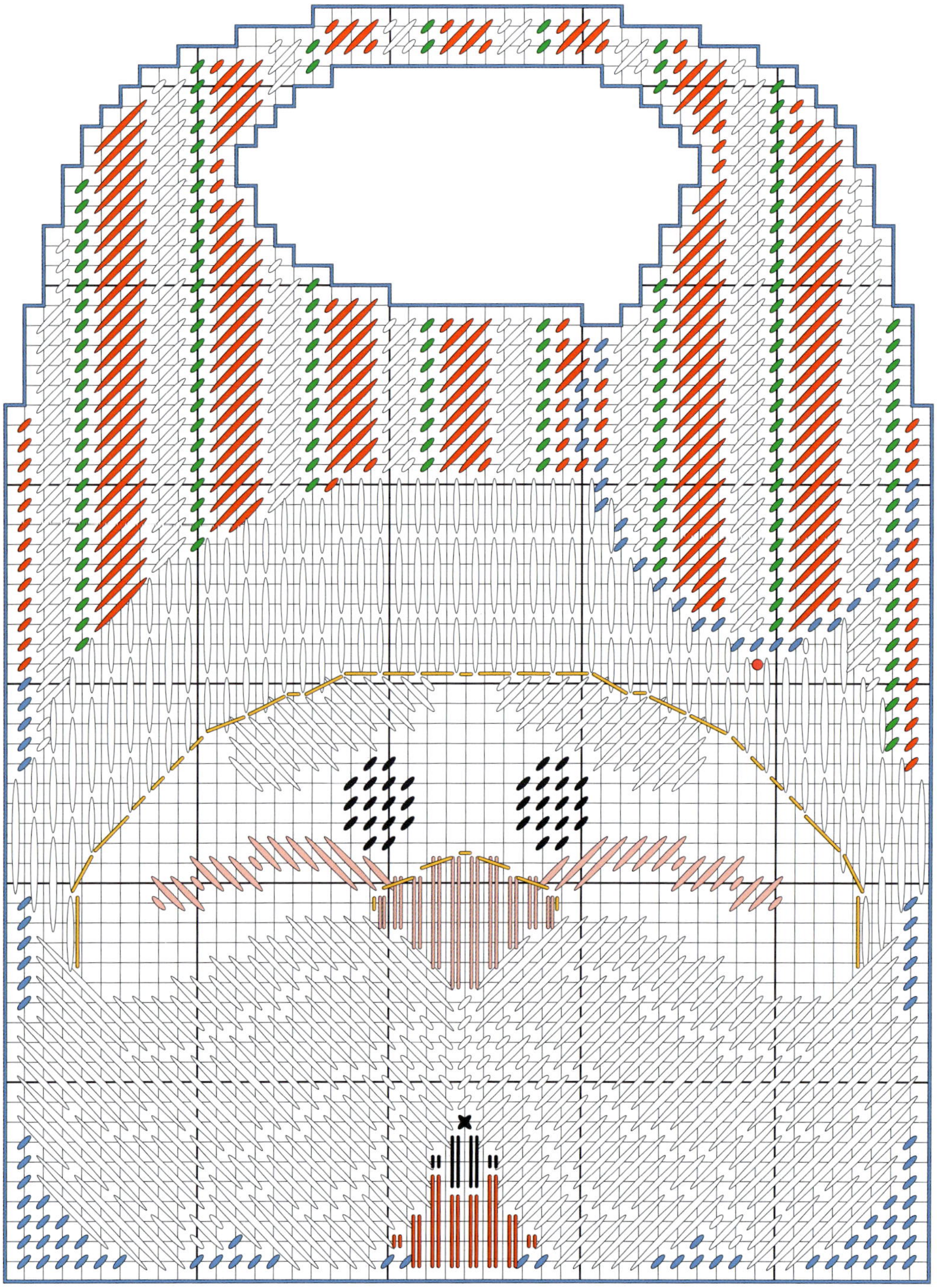

Santa Front/Back
48 holes x 64 holes
Cut 2 from stiff

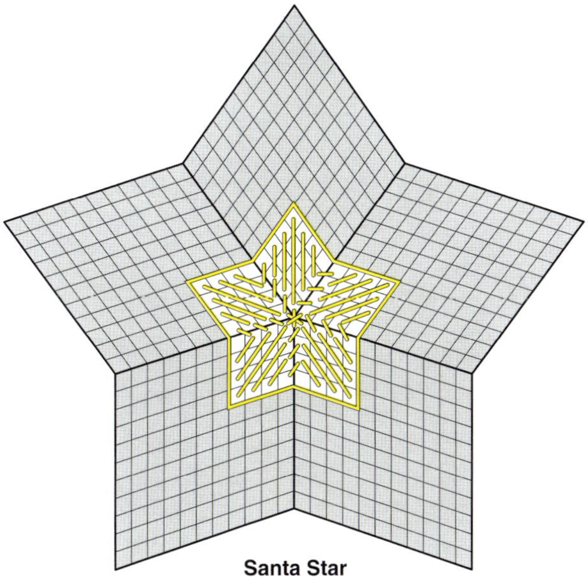

Santa Star
Cut 2 from 5-inch plastic canvas stars

COLOR KEY	
Yards	**Plastic Canvas Yarn**
2 (1.9m)	■ Black #00
12 (11m)	■ Red #01
35 (32m)	■ Burgundy #03
40 (36.6m)	□ White #41
5 (4.6m)	■ Watermelon #55
3 (2.8m)	■ Yellow #57
10 (9.2m)	Uncoded areas are light peach #56 Continental Stitches
	⁄ White #41 Straight Stitch
	Metallic Braid Ribbon
2 (1.9m)	■ Dark green #04 (4mm)
	6-Strand Embroidery Floss
3 (2.8m)	⁄ Very dark gray #3799 Backstitch and Straight Stitch
	● Attach jingle bell

Color numbers given are for Uniek Needloft plastic canvas yarn, Madeira GlissenGloss metallic braid ribbon and DMC embroidery floss.

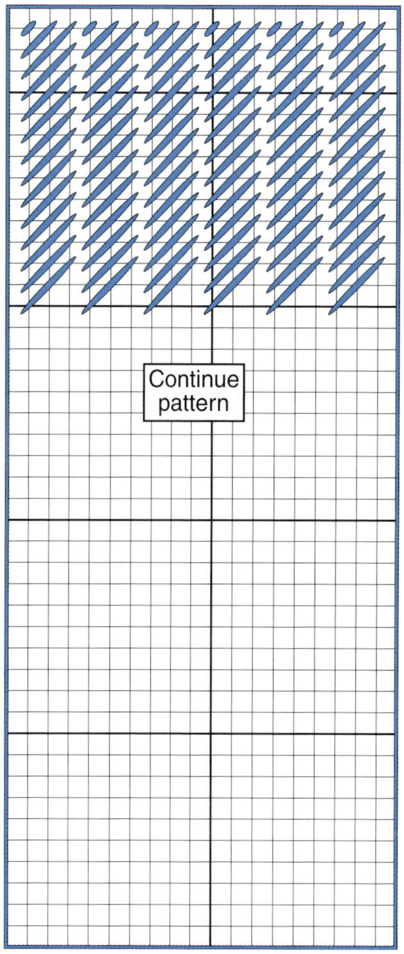

Santa Side
19 holes x 44 holes
Cut 2 from regular

Valentine Plaid

Size: 6 inches W x 8⅜ inches H x 3 inches D (15.2cm x 21.3cm x 7.6cm) excluding handles
Skill Level: Beginner

Materials

- ❑ 7-count plastic canvas from Darice:
  - ½ sheet clear regular
  - 1 sheet stiff
- ❑ 2 (6-inch/15.2cm) plastic canvas hearts from Darice
- ❑ Uniek Needloft plastic canvas yarn as listed in color key
- ❑ Madeira GlissenGloss 2mm and 4mm metallic braid ribbon as listed in color key
- ❑ 1 yard (1m) 1-inch-wide (2.5cm) pregathered white eyelet trim
- ❑ Tapestry needles: #16, #18
- ❑ Hot-glue gun

Stitching Step by Step

1 *Cut plastic canvas according to graphs:* Cut two sides from regular; two front/back pieces from stiff; and two hearts from plastic canvas hearts.

2 From regular plastic canvas, also cut two pieces 61 holes x 2 holes for handles, and one piece 39 holes x 19 holes for tote bottom; tote bottom will remain unstitched.

3 Stitch front, back and sides according to graphs, leaving unstitched areas along diagonal edges of front and back as noted, and filling in remaining uncoded areas with white Continental Stitches.

4 Stitch hearts using watermelon yarn according to graph.

5 When background stitching is complete, Straight Stitch over plaid design on front, back and sides using 2mm metallic braid ribbon. Work French Knots on hearts using white and red yarns. Overcast edges of hearts and work long Straight Stitches over cutout openings using 4mm metallic braid ribbon.

6 *Handles:* Thread one end of a 1¾-yard (2m) piece of red yarn through a hole in one end of a handle strip, leaving a short tail. Wrap handle evenly with red yarn, covering the tail with the first few wraps, and overlapping as you wrap to cover plastic canvas completely. Thread other end through last hole in other end of plastic canvas strip; thread under last few wraps. Repeat to cover remaining handle strip with 4mm metallic braid ribbon.

7 Referring to photo throughout, hot-glue eyelet trim around outer edge of hearts. Hot-glue ends of one handle strip to reverse side of heart, positioning ends at top center of each lobe. Repeat with remaining handle strip and heart.

8 Using white yarn throughout, Whipstitch front and back to sides along corners; Whipstitch tote bottom to front, back and sides. Overcast top edges of sides.

9 Hot-glue hearts to front and back of tote over unstitched areas.

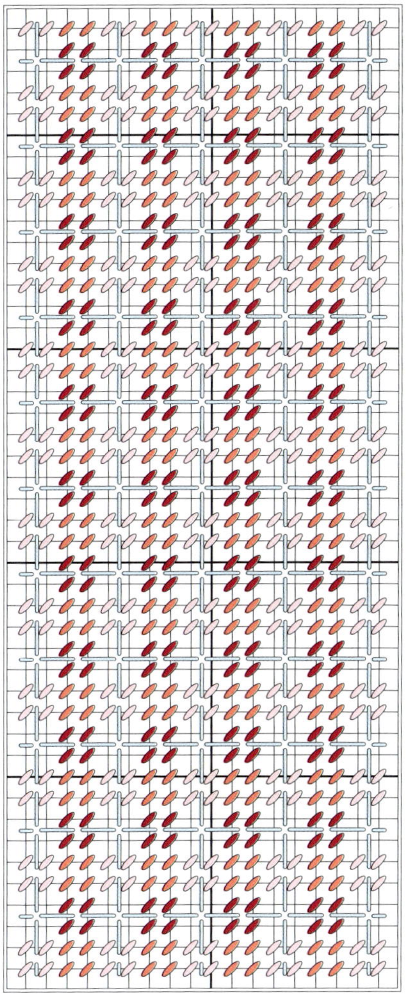

Valentine Plaid Side
19 holes x 46 holes
Cut 2 from regular

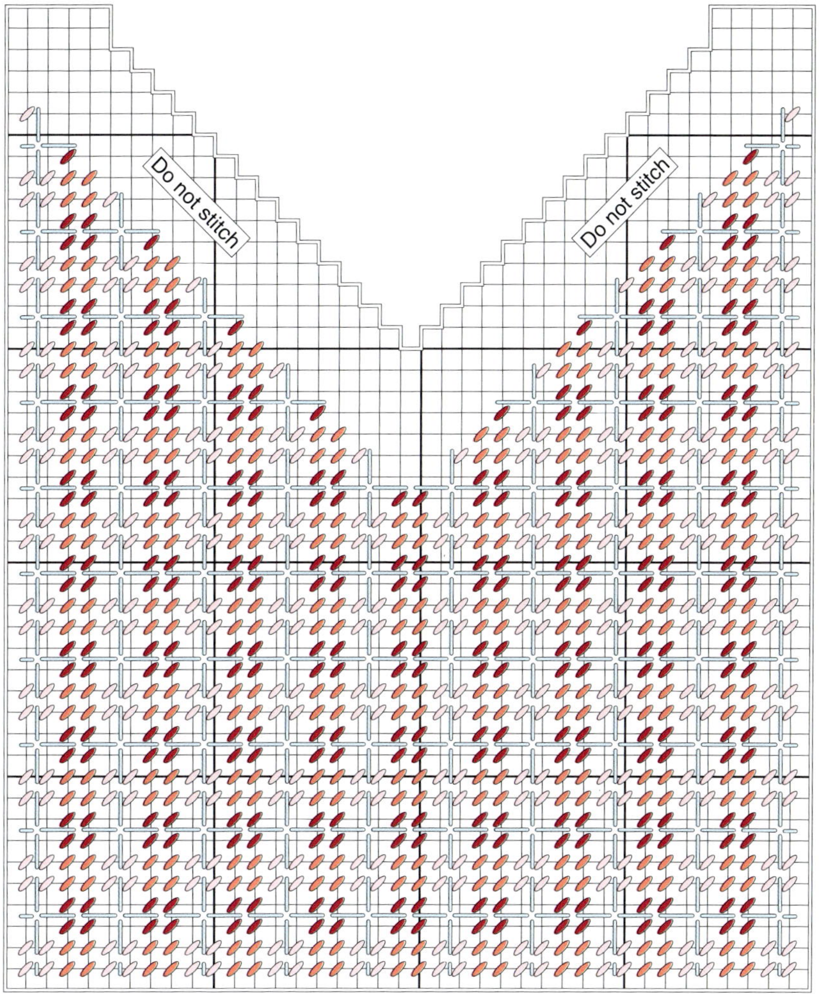

Valentine Plaid Front/Back
39 holes x 46 holes
Cut 2 from stiff

Valentine Plaid Heart
Cut 2 from 6-inch plastic canvas hearts

COLOR KEY

Yards	Plastic Canvas Yarn
24 (22m)	Red #01
25 (22.9m)	Pink #07
33 (30.2m)	Watermelon #55
50 (45.7m)	Uncoded areas on front/back and side are white #41 Continental Stitches
	White #41 Overcasting
	Watermelon #55 Straight Stitch
	Red #01 French Knot
	White #41 French Knot
	Metallic Braid Ribbon
38 (34.8m)	Silver #03 (2mm) Straight Stitch
16 (14.7m)	Silver #03 (4mm) Straight Stitch and Overcast

Color numbers given are for Uniek Needloft plastic canvas yarn and Madeira GlissenGloss metallic braid ribbon.

The full line of The Needlecraft Shop products is carried by Annie's Attic catalog.

TOLL-FREE ORDER LINE
or to request a free catalog
(800) 582-6643
Customer Service
(800) 449-0440
Fax (800) 882-6643
Visit AnniesAttic.com

ISBN: 978-1-57367-281-8
Printed in USA
2 3 4 5 6 7 8 9

Shopping for Supplies

For supplies, first shop your local craft and needlework stores. Some supplies may be found in fabric, hardware and discount stores. If you are unable to find the supplies you need, please call Annie's Attic at (800) 259-4000 to request a free catalog that sells plastic canvas supplies.

Getting Started

Before You Cut

Buy one brand of canvas for each entire project, as brands can differ slightly in the distance between bars. Count holes carefully from the graph before you cut, using the bolder lines that show each 10 holes. These 10-mesh lines begin in the lower left corner of each graph to make counting easier. Mark canvas before cutting, then remove all marks completely before stitching. If the piece is cut in a rectangular or square shape and is either not worked, or worked with only one color and one type of stitch, we do not include the graph in the pattern. Instead, we give the cutting and stitching instructions in the general instructions or with the individual project instructions.

Covering the Canvas

Bring needle up from back of work, leaving a short length of yarn on back of canvas; work over short length to secure. To end a thread, weave needle and thread through the wrong side of your last few stitches; clip. Follow the numbers on the small graphs beside each stitch illustration; bring your needle up from the back of the work on odd numbers and down through the front of the work on even numbers. Work embroidery stitches last, after the canvas has been completely covered by the needlepoint stitches.

Basic Stitches

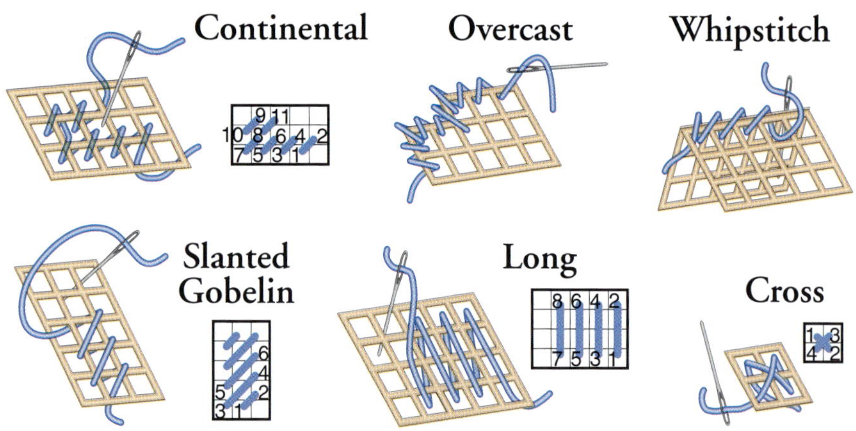

Embroidery Stitches

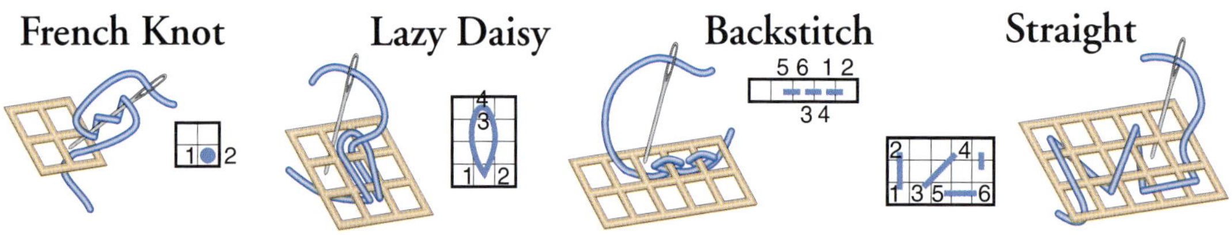

METRIC KEY:
millimeters = (mm)
centimeters = (cm)
meters = (m)
grams = (g)